The Dream Walker Awakens

'Astakdh Sa'ir Al Ahlam'

C. R. Puente

Dedication

To the soul who was worth bonding to.
forgiving, and loving despite all.
To the love that chose me,
and chooses me every single day.
To my God who gave me incredible gifts,
loves and forgives me no matter when I fall.

Preface

Soul Bonds exist and they are not easy to bear.
Overcome each other's weakness, Soul Bonds are spiritually
aware.
Unified as more than one, their bond cannot be destroyed.
Love is another dimension with them, they feel with their
souls conjoined.
Balance takes effort, talents and gifts may expound.
Open channels of emotions, they become more endowed.
Navigating life together is always a blessing and adventure.
Discovering what fate has in store for them with complete
awe and wonder.

Acknowledgements

As surely as the sun rises in the east,
Friends that are true are exceedingly rare.
Dedicated to the other half of my soul,
Advising without any praise to be given.
Listen to learn, laugh in the process,
Supporting each other through trials with prayer.
Advising without judgement, sharing without
boundaries,
Developing together throughout this transition.
Imparting shared thoughts through stories untold,
Quietly hoping to bring light to the world.

A Girl From The West

Although her family was from the other side of the sea in the west,
Germany was where a girl was born, with a voice that could scream above the rest.
Interestingly enough, the outside persona showed parents who loved that girl beyond belief.
Regrettably, few learned how horrible they treated her behind closed doors whenever she caused them grief.
Later, they'd find she'd been given incredible gifts from above.
'Favored by God' they'd say, whenever she sang or made art or gave gifts full of love.
Raising such a talented yet headstrong child proved more than her parents could handle.
Observing how the girl began having dreams and nightmares, they knew would cause a scandal.
Motivated by fear of what she might've become over time,
They had her locked up and heavily drugged, like she had committed some crime.

Hollow and empty the poor girl became, till she felt she
was old enough to go live on her own.
Exasperated her parents became because to them, she
would never be grown.
While she fought to break free, the dreams and
nightmares never diminished.
Ever fighting her parents and fighting her demons left
her strength unreplenished.
Surprised when one day, a man came to take her away,
yet it wasn't the fairytale she dreamed.
Through ever greater trials that girl fought for a while
and on her own, began trucking across Americas great
scene.

The First Soul Bond

Through the entire life of that girl, she always dreamed
of a blonde-haired, blue-eyed boy.
Her first dream with him, she watched him learn to ride
a bike, but he was hurt by the red truck of some cowboy.
Evidently, she dreamed of his grandmother too, with
short grey, curly hair and a contagious smile.
For years she watched him grow alongside her, even
watched him break his arm when he tried to fly.
It happened one day when she was pulling a load to a
guard shack where a familiar face stood.
Resisting the urge to believe, the boy now a grown man,
was who she'd watched in dreams all her childhood.
Surprise would hit her when she saw the scar on his face
and when he admitted where he got it from,
Took a few days for realization to hit and admit he was
her soul bond and feelings for him soon succumbed.
So quickly she fell for the man she had watched grow up
alongside her in her dreams,
Obviously never expected that soon he would bring
nightmares that would wake her with screams.

Unknowing she was, of his intolerable hatred of other
races,
Loving turned to sorrow as she witnessed his atrocities
in hidden places.
Bound as she had been, changed when she saw what he
did through his victims' eyes,
Observing their pain at his hands, never believing when
she questioned him of his lies.
Never wanting to be a part of the darkness that took
over his heart,
Damaged and torn, she left him alone for the sake of her
soul and a fresh start.

Dream Walker Awakens

Despite a life of hardships and pain, that girl grew
hopeful and full of light,
Refusing to give in to the darkness in her dreams, for her
sanity, she'd always have to fight.
Eventually realizing that the dreams were not a curse but
a gift,
Aligning the forces that be, now offered the chance for
her ability to shift.
Meaningless suddenly had meaning as dreams became
future tense,
Walking in dreams of others, to her, seemed to make
very little sense.
Allowed to see only a snip of people she'd meet, where
she'd end up, or of something that would happen,
Leaving a puzzle in her mind that would leave her
exhausted and her heart saddened.
Keeping her gift a secret, for exposing it made her seem
highly unstable,
Ever changing, her dreams, kept her weary as most were
uninterpretable.

Remembering the blonde boy whose prejudice and anger
would hurt without thought,
Absolving to only use her gifts to help others where she
could, no matter how much of her it would cost.
Wanting to believe in the goodness of others as her
dream paths ever changed,
Acclimating herself to life on her own yet her dreams
often left her from others estranged.
Keeping faith in God that He'd given her these gifts for a
reason,
Ever fighting the dreams in her mind left her in a
constant state of depletion.
Navigating a new lease on life with a gift, by her,
completely misunderstood,
She would begin a new adventure of her own by starting
a new trucking livelihood.

Man From The East

Many years ago, in a city across the sea by the shores of
the Euphrates River,
Asleep on a cot in a darkened room upstairs where the
desert night air made him shiver.
Not knowing a blast from the war just over his countries
border would wake with devastation.
Failing to understand the cost of their actions, his
brother and uncles would perish as victims of
assassination.
Realizing their home was no more, he and his family
became refugees and left their home shattered,
Only to be stuck in a refugee camp for years, treated
worse, like they didn't even matter.
Managing to get sent to the US where others lived free
from such tyranny,
Tearing up when he greeted his family from Michigan
knowing they were safe from such villainy.
Headstrong and stubborn, the boy became a man and
fought for a life to be proud of that he'd want.
Eventually settling down himself with a wife and kids

and even built his own restaurant.
Employing some family to take over while he was forced
to go back overseas,
Allowed greed to set in their hearts, they stole almost all
he had because they couldn't agree.
Suffering a massive loss, he moved his family to Texas to
reside and start anew,
Trying to build a new life as a trucker, away from his
kids, he missed them as they grew.

The Second Soul Bond

The third day at a new job she met a handsome man
with a foreign Eastern name.
Having no clue as to why, she felt she should be on her
knees in front of him all the same.
Ever since that day, she felt conflicted and constantly out
of sorts.
Seeking to understand why not kneeling before this man
would cause her some remorse.
Eventually years passed and their conversations became
more animated and sincere.
Considering all they talked about, it was without
judgements, boundaries, or fear.
Outside of work she met another who wanted nothing
more than forever and her heart.
Navigating the dating scene led to the inevitable shot by
Cupid's dart.
Despite her guy friend not wanting her to marry so
soon,
She gave herself away and tried not to think of dreams
on her honeymoon.

Observing new boundaries, they rarely except for work
spoke.
Unbeknownst to either of them, a couple years later her
gift through him awoke.
Leaving her breathless in dreams, she bonded to him in
the deepest sense.
Becoming more than the first bond and became so much
more intense.
Observing that once she bonded to him, even the dark
color of her eyes changed.
Never had that happened before and without the bond
could not be explained.
Discovering new levels of depth to her gift, it grew even
more than could be gauged.

Sa' ir Al Ahlam Is Born

She dreamed of his deepest fears in the nightmare that
haunted his very existence,
Aside him in his home, she watched as he checked every
window and door as safety was insistent.
Inside every room, she'd watch him, as he tensely looked
for anything amiss,
Reliving his fears as her own in this dream was not
something she could dismiss.
As he finished his rounds and sat at the table with his
gun under his leg,
Lightning lit up the apartment as his mate came in and
asked him to come back to bed.
Alarms went off in his head as he grabbed and threw her
to the floor,
Hearing the exact moment, he loaded the gun and aimed
at the men as they crashed through the door.
Leaving no man alive and reloading to make sure they
were all dead,
A sound escaped his throat that would fill that girl with
dread.

Moments passed in the blink of an eye, and she woke,
her face covered in tears,
If this was his nightmare that haunted him so, then she
completely understood his fears.
She asked him the next day if indeed he did dream and
the truth to her was what he told:
"Believe me, I saw you there beside me, fighting by my
side as their bodies grew cold."
Offering comfort to him, in the place where they dream
things they cannot imagine,
Reassuring him he doesn't have to fight alone and
offered him her strength and compassion.
Now he understood that she walked in his dreams and
was truly a part of his soul.

Sa'ir Al Ahlam

Seeking through the freezing cold of the blackness or the
raging fires burning heat,

A light with a purpose to find, her cut out heart as a
guide in her hand beat.

Ignoring the smell of burning flesh and puddles of blood
to reach her goal,

Resisting the dark to stay on the path that would lead
her to the other half of her soul.

Although the depth of her sacrifice, ages lost, would be
remembered by his ancestors she'd meet.

Love would lead her through the depths of his hell as
she'd forgiven him the sins she was shown,

Arriving at the tent of his ancient family line in the
depths of hell, he'd never have known.

His disbelief grew upon seeing her and the extent of the
gift she had given in her hand.

Loving him despite the darkness of this hell and finding
him against all odds in the sand,

Awoke in them both a bond forged through the gift that
would see them both through.

Made sacred through sacrifice and the purest love, she
became his *Rafiq Alrouh.*

Awakens Rafiq Alrouh

Assessing this new bond with the guy from the east and
all their shared dreams entailed,
Whatever the bond brought for the both of them, she
offered the promise to him she wouldn't fail.
As sure as the sun rose every morning, every dream she
shared with him turned her eyes gold,
Keeping them green, her eyes, when her dreams bits of
the future foretold.
Even sharing those dreams was too much for him to try
to understand,
Never really knowing if she spoke the truth, sometimes
felt out of hand.
Seeing no lie from her when he questioned her and saw
the truth in her eyes,
Realizing he cared for her deeply despite being married
meant they'd have to live a lie.
Acknowledging the fact of the bond meant believing in
more than what was written,
Facing the truth of the bond and learning all it entailed,
surely must not be forbidden.

Inspiration grew within them both as she thought each
had accepted their bonds entirely,
Questions remained even though her gifts already
present, grew exponentially.
Aside from the questions that inside him still grew,
Localizing his feelings for her, he kept his emotions hid
so that no one knew.
Realizing that resisting the bond only caused heartache
and grief,
Obeying the call of the bond brought her a renewed
sense of joy and relief.
Unlike the bond she was born with, she witnessed what
he saw when his eyes she looked through.
However it happened and for whatever reason, she was
learning what it meant to be *Rafiq Alrouh*.

Resisting The Bond

Regret seeped into his heart although he did not mean
for it to become known,
Especially considering his mate, he didn't think his
feelings for that girl should've grown.
Scrutinizing every detail of that girl as he tended to
seriously overthink things,
Insisted his head over his heart that maybe he should
end things before they begin.
Sitting alone more often than not as he stared blankly at
the computer screen,
Tackled by thoughts of 'is it right or is it wrong' made
his head hurt more than the damn machine.
Immersing himself in his work and his job to try to keep
his heart quiet,
Navigating his daily life with her and his family often
affected his diet.
Gambling had become something of a way to escape the
everyday bore,
Taking his shot at the stock market showed promise and
he knew he wanted even more.

Hesitating to accept the bond with her gave him reason
to work on this new pursuit,
Every so often, he even put their conversations on mute.
Before she ever told him of what her side of the bond
could be like,
Omitting the fact that she had no idea what *Rafiq Alrouh*
was, caused him to act out of spite.
Not wanting to admit he had a connection to that girl
was causing him problems,
Dare he think there was more to this that could make
this relationship blossom?

Sa'ir Al Ahlam Asking

Sensing his reluctance to accept the truth of what her
capabilities were and are,
At first, she considered asking the ones she'd seen in his
dreams, no matter how bizarre.
Imagining no other way and hoping it wouldn't offend
her or his God,
Respecting his beliefs, she would ask for nothing but
clarity, no matter if the idea was flawed.
As she drifted off to sleep, she kept one question she held
in her open mind,
Leaving the now behind, she hoped she'd be answered by
any of his kind.
Against the coarseness of the sand, she found herself on
her knees in the dream,
Her cut out heart was still in her left hand, and she held
it up for all of them to see.
Light came from behind the group surrounding her that
seemed to be all women,
Assuming they were from his tribe, all veiled and
covered from head to toe in dark linen.

Muttering and whispering amongst themselves as a pale
light behind them shown,
Assuming it was the language of his tribe for to her, it
was completely unknown.
Surprised they were when she showed them the gift in
her hand that she 'd given,
Know they did the great significance when a heart from
your chest is freely riven.
Inviting yet keeping a distance, she kept hearing the
same set of words yet to her they had no meaning.
Nevertheless, as she awoke, they'd leaned forward and
whispered the answer she was needing.
Giving that girl the answer for what she had asked for,
they called her "the girl who bleeds".

Forbidden Passion For Her

Forging a passion for that girl started way back at the
beginning,
On the first day he met her, his head was lost in her
features and his heart was swimming.
Regret was momentary as their relationship and bond
grew over time,
Besides her stance, poise and charisma, it all made him
get lost in her eyes.
Interestingly enough, he had watched how her eyes had
changed from brown to green to gold,
Deep in his heart he knew she was special and admitting
his attraction, crossed a new threshold.
Deciding to take the leap, despite the obvious objections,
Encouraged by her willingness to submit, he stared into
her eyes at his reflection.
Needing to voice no request, he touched he face and
gently kissed her lips,
Passion took over as she yielded to him and his hands
grabbed her hips.
Allowing him to possess her mouth, she opened her

arms to him and allowed him inside,
Savoring the taste of her and the warmth of all of her, for
him, she would never deny.
Sliding his tongue into her mouth to become one with
her on every level imaginable,
Immersing himself into her light and love showed him
how her heart was so charitable.
Occupying her body with his, sent his heat racing and
his mind soaring,
Needless to say, the passion ignited soon had him to the
edge nearing.
Feeling her need as his own left his mind reeling,
Opening himself to her completely, almost had him on
the ground, kneeling.
Riding the skies with her would feel like heaven to him,
Her body wrapped around his, had his heart full to the
brim.
Electrified bodies, hammering pulses, and hearts
intertwined,
Reflecting love for him in her eyes as their souls were
now completely entwined.

Forbidden Passion For Him

Feeling his desire for her without ever uttering a single
word needing spoken,
Observing his eyes darken as he reached to touch her
face, her eyes wide open.
Resisting him not as he touched his lips to hers and she
silently asked him to lead her,
Breathing his scent as she wrapped her arms around
him, inviting him deeper.
Igniting a blaze from way deep inside her as he dove
deep into her mouth,
Deeper and deeper she opened up and let him explore, to
his will she bowed.
Dazzling the senses was what the taste and feel and
smell of him did to her,
Enveloping him with her body, she gave willingly as she
started to purr.
Nibbling his neck and feeling his hands grab her hips,
she openly complied,
Pausing for just a second to feel his heat, she heard from
his chest a deep sigh.

Awaiting the question directed by his lightest touch,
So gentle yet firm, to go over the edge would take just a nudge.
Seeing pure exstacy on his face as he buried himself into the heat of her body,
Igniting a fire between them was like drinking the sweetest yet darkest hot coffee.
On the edge of her seat he kept teasing, their heartrates began to increase.
New feelings and emotions pulled new sensations through the bond, something like peace.
For after he poured his breath into her, she felt how the bond became deeper, more rooted,
Opposite their bodies sway, separate then together they moved, ridged yet fluid.
Racing hearts as they fight to catch their breath, their beating hearts slowed,
Her body, her mind, her heart, and her soul now echoed with the love that on her face, now showed.
Immersing himself into her had brought them both a sense of total completion,
Mirrored in his eyes was her love for him and now it didn't matter the reason.

Living Two as One

Leaving doubt behind her as her resolve in their bond
grew even more,
Involved with him in every aspect had created through
the bond, an open door.
Visions increased of his daily activities, his dreams, and
even heated discussions,
Instances included seeing through his eyes in real time;
those her life interrupted.
Never imagining the bond was capable of such crazy
things,
Got even more strange when she could taste the exact
moment when he was smoking.
Together in every part of the word was something more
than either of them could have imagined,
Wondering why fate or their God had brought them
together in such a fashion.
Organizing their thoughts to keep things from getting
out of hand, with him held the utmost importance.
Assuring him that she meant no harm to him or his
family, she'd promise not to be a disturbance.

Seeing, feeling, tasting, and hearing his life through this
bond seemed too much for him to handle,
Observing this way had simply become easier for her,
she never meant to cause a scandal.
Nevertheless, she could feel that something from him
was deeply amiss,
Eluding her with his sudden silence, she had no idea he
was about to drop her into an abyss.

Trying To Break The Bond

Treating the bond like it was some kind of threat or
nuisance,
Risking not his marriage or his faith for that girl or her
impudence.
Yearnings for her were wrong in the deepest sense of his
religion,
Insisting the truth that girl said, the bond she tried to get
him to believe in.
Needing to know if it could be done, he quit that girl and
their conversations,
Guilt plagued him but he stayed silent and never offered
her an explanation.
Temptations he kept out of his mind as he sought to do
the unthinkable,
Outside of his family, only she knew, he thought the
bond was completely mythical.
Bound to destroy what didn't exist, because he couldn't
for his sake, believe in it,
Regret pushed aside, he tried, and he tried to undo and
make the bond nonexistent.

Eventually feeling successful in his endeavor, he felt
confident this was the right decision,
Acquiring funds to keep his family happy and safe
became his one and only ambition.
Knowing not what caused the pain or why he would
allow it to happen,
Tears streaked down her face as she woke in more pain
than she could've imagined.
Hollow and empty, the bond felt like the inside was
jagged, ripped, burnt, and torn,
Enough to leave her sobbing for air, her chest felt like it
was wrapped in thorns.
Balance was distorted, as everything in the nightmare
became her reality,
Oblivious he was of the pain he had caused her when for
his own sake, he acted rashly.
Negating the fact that the bond was hers and not his,
would be up to her for the unbinding,
Despite whatever she felt from him; she would forgive
and keep her heart pure and shining.

Afflicting Dreams and Nightmares

Apart from the pain that radiated through the bond and
how it affected her life,
Forced that girl to accept that this is how she would have
to live, every breath filled with knives.
Fathoming not why she would be in so much pain every
waking moment,
Lamenting their friendship that was, now he seemed to
her, an opponent.
Impacted by pain, she ignored anyway, she continued to
be courageous and kind,
Caring for him would never change and to his silence,
herself she resigned.
Then when night fell, her dreams slowly descended into
hellish and freakishly real dreams,
Immobilizing her with fear, she awoke unable to move;
sometimes woke silently screaming.
Now and again, they would have to do with the agony
that her shadow dealt,
Glimpsing through the eyes of his victims and all the

pain he was causing, she felt.
Dangerous and daring he had become, not seeming to
care wether or not he got caught,
Relief she felt, when someone told her he'd been
arrested, in jail she was shown; and she watched.
Easing those fears that he would escape to hurt someone
purely out of spite,
Approaching each day cautiously, almost afraid to heave
a healing sigh.
Managing to reconnect with her bonded when he saw
something about her had become very wrong,
Seeking to find an answer as to why she was no longer
happy or singing her favorite songs.
Admitting that maybe he had done something to hurt
her wasn't a comforting thought,
Normalizing a simple friendship was more of what he
thought she would want.
Didn't want to hear of dreams or the bond or else it
would make him disappear,
Negotiating with him daily so that the rules he put forth
were never unclear.
Insisting still that she meant him no harm and wanted
nothing from him,
Gave him daily reminders of how awesome he was and
found reasons to make him grin.
However, it happened so slowly for sure, they became
better friends and chatted daily,

Trying not to remember the nightmares caused by her
shadow when they happened nightly.
Maintaining their relationships with their respective
partners came first,
Aided their own bonds to grow and become more
reinforced.
Recognizing how to grow together and adapt to new
challenges,
Eradicated most of their problems and it erased almost
all of life's imbalances.
Strengthened by his resolve, care, and concern, she'd
follow her bond while through life they navigated.

Accepting His Rafiq Alrouh

As time went by, she spoke of her dreams and he
listened to help still her fears,
Caring more for each other while navigating their bonds,
made them kind of like pioneers.
Comforting each other when life in its unfairness threw
them horrible curve balls,
Encouraged and celebrated their goals met and wins for
each other, no matter how small.
Pivotal moments in each of their lives when he finally
accepted her for who she was,
Though it may seem unfair to his mate or her partner,
neither suffered for there was no facade.
Honored their spouses they did as well as pour their
hearts into the bond,
Interesting enough, they could share each other's passion
when to their partners they made love.
Senses exploded in every way, the more they accepted
each other and grew,
Responding through bonds became second nature, it was
as if the other already knew.

Astounding at first but then it became clear,
For the stronger the emotion, the other knew as if they
were near.
In other instances, she dreamed of others and when she
asked them of their lives,
Quickly they answered what it was she had dreamed of,
wether exciting or strife.
Amassing some bravery when she thought they should
try something new,
Laid a hand on her heart and cleared her mind through.
Rafiq Alrouh was repeated three times and instantly
there was a connection,
Outside of herself and yet deep from within, she felt his
deepest affections.
Unlike anything else in this world, was what connected
them through the bond,
Having a spiritual way to communicate, share emotions,
see, and even respond.

Sinister Plot Unfolds

Sometimes in her sleep, when awakened by the most
horrible dreams and nightmares,
Inflicted on her were the plans of her shadow as he tried
to intimidate and scare.
Not wanting to tell her partner or her bonded the details
of all she was shown,
Instead, she began a diary of sorts, to keep track in case
one day it became known.
Seeing her torn apart by things she couldn't control,
broke both her bonded and her partner's heart.
Trusting that both of them would support her, she threw
her pain into great works of art.
Every so often she'd dream of the evil things her shadow
would try to do,
Realizing that these paths shown, were things she was
about to go through.
Preventing disaster didn't seem to be a choice so she
knew she'd better prepare,
Loved she did, so many, and she didn't want them to
worry or become aware.

Of all the things she was shown, there was only one terrible outcome,
To try and prevent this thing was crazy so instead, she'd get things ready for when the time comes.
Utilizing all of her strength to put certain ideas into motion,
Never revealing the truth of the matter to anyone, lest it cause a commotion.
Fabricating and selling her art became an absolute dream come true,
Obtaining necessary means to prepare to do all that she needed to do.
Loving her partner, her bonded, her God and her family knowing that her time was precious,
Doing all she could do as her dreams had shown her, and how to escape her nemesis.
Sending prayers to the One, that He could help her with all in her dreams, previewed.

That Girl Was Shot

That nemesis of hers, the blonde man with blue eyes,
never forgave her for loving and then leaving him,
He watched her over the years as she moved on, became
successful, and also married another man.
Actively seeking her over the internet, he plotted and
planned till he could escape,
Tore him apart to see her with men who were not him,
and her friends who were not of his race.
Given the chance at parole, he waited till he acquired all
that he needed,
In finding her next debut at an art show would give him
access to her, unheeded.
Resenting the men she was with, had him blinded by
rage and a need for revenge,
Lying in wait for the perfect moment when she was
alone to give her a present.
Waltzing up to her side when the men left to attend
other things as she directed,
Astonishment written on her face when her shadow she
recognized, and she knew his objective.

Suspense filled the air as he drew from his jacket a gun
and madly at her, began to shout,
She smiled sadly at him and stood her ground as her
bonded and her partner tried to find a way out.
Her shadow saw that guy and the way he was dressed
and tried to take aim at him instead,
Optimistic she was as she threw insults at him until he
turned to her and fired his gun at her head.
Trying to protect the ones she loves; she gave her life as
her love poured out.

Fly Rafiq Alrouh

Flinging himself onto his family, her bonded watched as
she fell to the floor,
Launching himself at her attacker, her shadow was
disabled though the whole time he swore.
Yelling atrocities at them all until the sirens were heard
in the distance,
Realizing she was dying, they all stopped and tried to
offer their assistance.
As she looked into the faces of both her partner and her
soul bond,
Fighting to hold on to tell them all the love she had for
them, and then she was gone.
Into his arms her partner held her and wept while that
guy ran outside,
Quiet was what he sought even though his family and
everyone stood crying inside.
Although his mate knew how deeply he cared for that
girl without ever saying,
Lamenting his actions, she knew, he would his entire life
let this memory betray him.

Recalling everything that girl had said about how deeply
they were bonded,
Outside, he cleared his mind and called *Rafiq Alrouh*
three times and hoped that she'd respond.
Unlike before, when he called her this way, he felt more
than anything he could've imagined,
Having her answer beyond deaths door, brought joy and
peace and his heart was no longer saddened.

Living As More Than One

Leaving either of them without her was not what she
wanted form the start,
Investing herself into her art was the only way to ensure
they would never, from her part.
Ventured into prospects for the future where she knew
she would not be in it,
Involved trips to a lawyer and prepaid cremation, in case
her nightmares were legit.
Not wanting to leave her partner in financial distress or
need,
Gave him access to every sale of her art unsold, to him
she gave the deed.
As for the other half of her soul, she never really left his
side,
Since the moment he called her after her death, every
time he called, she replied.
Made a way she had, to keep in trust until the time was
right that he'd need,
Oblivious he'd been to her plans, yet she did everything
she could to help him succeed.

Relief was what he felt when he called *Rafiq Alrouh*
three times,
Enabling this form of connection was communication
where she could help and guide.
Two they were as one, now living with only space
between them,
Heaven would have to wait for the one, till the other
eyes are seen once again.
Assured her bonded was, that she would stay for as long
as she was needed,
Now and again, she would check on her partner and
make sure that he was well treated.
Observing her partner and her bonded helped them to
know she would always love them both,
Navigating life with only her presence was how to them,
she kept her oath.
Everlasting love she poured out for those she cherished
till their time on Earth was completed.

Heaven Sent Rafiq Alrouh

Having her near made the rest of life's journey easier to
navigate,
Every hardship and challenge, he heard words of
encouragement whispered, none too late.
As fast as time flew by, no longer a parent but now a
grandfather,
Victorious his life had been in living his life until he
could go no farther.
Eventually he slowed down and he knew his time would
soon be over,
Not forgetting his bonded and all she did for him with all
that had been shown her.
Setting up plans so his family would never be without,
Never one to waste with the memory of the war that he
had come out of,
Trusting that each of them would see these as acts of
pure love.
Radiating warmth through the bond, he felt that girl was
near,
Affirming that it was about time to go, for she knows

being gifted as a seer.
For in her journal, she had spelled out disasters as she
was shown that it would happen,
Interesting were other dreams written she'd had, were
more than anyone could've ever imagined.
Questions arose but her final letter said for everyone to
trust in God above,
Always to remember that this was all His will, and our
lives and gifts were to show His love.
Luminating the darkness was all that girl tried to do with
her art, her love and her life,
Rafiq Alrouh he was and as he repeated the beloved
phrase the third and final time.
Overjoyed he was when she appeared by his side,
encased in pure white light.
Unhindered by the body that no longer imprisoned him,
his soul began to take flight.
Hand in hand they left this place far behind, as up to the
heavens they climbed.

www.ingramcontent.com/pod-product-compliance
Lightning Source LLC
La Vergne TN
LVHW021305200726
843509LV00012B/1783